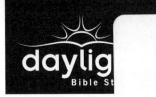

A DVD-based study series
Study Guide

LAND OF CONFLICT

An Arab and Jewish Conversation

A DVD-based study series
Study Guide

LAND OF CONFLICT

An Arab and Jewish Conversation

With Mart De Haan

Eight Lessons for Group Exploration

DISCOVERY HOUSE

P U B L I S H E R S ®

Feeding the Soul with the Word of God

The DayLight Bible Studies are based on programs produced by
Day of Discovery, a Bible-teaching TV series of RBC Ministries.

© 2011 by Discovery House Publishers

Discovery House Publishers is affiliated with RBC Ministries,
Grand Rapids, Michigan.

Requests for permission to quote from this book should be directed to:

Permissions Department
Discovery House Publishers
P.O. Box 3566
Grand Rapids, MI 49501

All Scripture quotations, unless otherwise indicated, are taken from the
HOLY BIBLE, NEW INTERNATIONAL VERSION®. NIV®
Copyright © 1973, 1978, 1984 by Biblica, Inc. ™
Used by permission of Zondervan.
All rights reserved worldwide.
www.zondervan.com

Study questions by Andrew Sloan
Interior design by Sherri L. Hoffman
Cover design by Jeremy Culp

ISBN: 978-1-57293-519-8

Printed in the United States of America

11 12 13 14 / 10 9 8 7 6 5 4 3 2 1

CONTENTS

INTRODUCTION

Behold the Possibilities

Things can change when good people talk with and listen to each other.

We've all watched as two sides in a heated conflict battled over a clash of opinions or beliefs. If those sides see each other as mortal enemies with no hope of resolution, nothing positive comes from the conflict. We see this sometimes in the realm of government when people on opposing sides of the political fence refuse to listen to each other to seek common ground.

But if two opposing sides could look at each other as important equals with valuable opinions and backgrounds—and with a dedication to love and civility, perhaps the two sides could come to an agreement about how to interact.

That is the hopeful approach that could take hold if two groups who share the land of Israel could find enough common ground to stop fighting and start co-existing as fellow citizens.

Behold the possibilities if folks of Arab decent and folks of Jewish decent could talk together about their differences with reason and respect.

That is exactly what happened on a small scale when the *Day of Discovery* film crew visited with two citizens of Israel: Avner Boskey and Nizar Touma. With RBC Ministries president Mart De Haan as the facilitator, these two remarkable gentlemen discussed with civility and mutual respect some of the toughest questions that face two men of such divergent backgrounds.

Avner Boskey is Jewish, a resident of Beersheba who has served in the Israeli army, who has studied theology in the United States, and who is a student of his country's history, culture, and religions. Nizar Touma is Arab, a citizen who lives in Israel and pastors a church in Nazareth. One Jewish, one Arab—but both brothers. Brothers because of their shared faith in the Lord Jesus Christ.

Together, they and Mart visited several locations in the land promised to Avner's ancestors—which in and of itself could be a source of contention in their discussions—to discuss both their differences and their similarities.

Remarkably, the two men go beyond the emotion of the difficult questions Mart asks them. And even more remarkably, what passes between these two sons of Abraham is a clear respect and a refreshing brotherly love.

This Arab-Jewish conversation, hosted by an American—in addition to providing fascinating answers to tough questions—sets forth hope that with the right spirit and the right understanding two factions that have historically been at odds could one day live in unity.

Watch Avner and Nizar in action. And behold the possibilities.

—Dave Branon
Editor

Representing the Remnant

DAYLIGHT PREVIEW

Distant Sons of One Father

The contrast is amazing. Two men: Avner Boskey and Nizar Touma. One from southern Israel, living in the town of Abraham's well, Beersheba. Jewish by birth. A former Israeli soldier. A scholar. The other from northern Israel, living in the town where Jesus grew up, Nazareth. Palestinian by birth. A pastor. Both sons of Abraham, and now, by choice, followers of Jesus Christ. Christians who live in a land where they are expected to be enemies, yet they are brothers in Christ. Mart De Haan introduces these men to us as together they begin to have an Arab and Jewish conversation about following Jesus in a land of conflict.

COME TOGETHER

Icebreaker Questions

1. Literal walls and fences divide the Arab and Jewish residents of Israel. Did any geographical, social, or ethnic boundaries separate people in the community in which you grew up? How about in the community in which you live now?

2. Who was the peacemaker in your family when you were growing up?

3. When have you felt the most clearly like a minority?

 FINDING DAYLIGHT

Experience the Video

Feel free to jot down Video Notes as you watch the presentation by Mart De Haan, Avner Boskey, and Nizar Touma. Use the space below for those notes.

---VIDEO NOTES---

Citizens of Israel: Brothers in Christ

Avner Boskey

Nizar Touma

Church of the Lord's Prayer

Impact of the conflict: Jew vs. Arab

Nizar's three conflicts and the message

Avner's challenge because of faith

Identity problems

Political conflict and others

Christianity as anti-Semitic

Christian history and Judaism

WALKING IN THE DAYLIGHT

Discussion Time

──────────── DISCOVER GOD'S WORD ────────────

Discussion/Application Questions

1. What have been your perceptions of the conflict between the Jewish and Palestinian people?

2. Both Nizar Touma and Avner Boskey state that being a believer today in the Middle East, and especially in Israel, is very challenging. Like most Arabs living in Israel, Nizar classifies himself as a Palestinian by nationality. The great majority of Arabs in Israel are Muslims, though a small percentage consider themselves followers of Jesus. And among those who are in that category, the great majority see themselves as "traditional Christians" rather than born-again believers.

   a. What internal conflicts, pertaining to personal identity issues, would a Palestinian believer like Nizar face?

   b. What external conflicts, pertaining to social, religious, and political issues, would a Palestinian believer like Nizar face?

c. How would the fact that Palestinian believers are in continuous conflict in regard to politics and religion intensify the message of peace and salvation—particularly in the sense, as Nizar says, that "we cannot make it without Jesus"?

3. **In addition to being a Jew living in Israel, which is surrounded by often-hostile Muslim nations, Avner is a member of the minority community of messianic Jewish believers.**

a. What internal conflicts, pertaining to personal identity issues, would a messianic Jewish believer like Avner face?

b. What external conflicts, pertaining to social, religious, and political issues, would a messianic Jewish believer like Avner face?

c. How would the fact, as Avner says, that "the issue comes back to the Scriptures as the only foundation that either Jew or Arab living in this country can really hold on to" enable believers to cope with all these struggles?

4. Avner notes that a major obstacle to Jews responding to the gospel is the fact that they think of Christianity as being an anti-Semitic, or anti-Jewish, religion—which causes them to fear that believing in Jesus as Messiah will take away their identity.

   How accurate do you think that perception is?

5. Avner refers to a couple of points the apostle Paul made in Romans 9. Read Romans 9:1–5.

   a. Although Paul was "the apostle to the Gentiles" (Romans 11:13), how did he feel about his fellow Jews?

   b. What advantages did his fellow Jews have, even though they had not followed Jesus the Messiah?

6. Later in Romans 9, Paul talks about a "remnant" (v. 27), which consists of both Jews and Gentiles (v. 24)—the vast majority being Gentiles (vv. 30–31). Avner states that both he and Nizar represent a remnant of believers, one to the Jews and the other to the Arabs. And being the remnant means crying out for their people—pleading with God for a real breakthrough regarding the Messiah for their people; being willing, like Paul indicated in Romans 9:3, to die for their people.

Can you relate to the image and experience of being part of God's "remnant"? Can you relate to having a longing for the salvation of your people?

──────────── BRINGING IT HOME ────────────

1. Earlier you shared about your perceptions of the conflict between the Jewish and Palestinian people. How open are you to changing your perspective?

2. What do you hope to gain from this study and from spending time with this group?

DAYLIGHT ON PRAYER

Spending Time with God

1. Nizar states that every person has some kind of internal conflict. How can the group support you in prayer in the midst of your conflicts or struggles?

2. Do you have any other prayer requests to share with the group?

DAYLIGHT AHEAD

Which "side" are you on? Are followers of Christ supposed to take sides in the Arab-Jewish conflict, or is there a better way to look at this ancient yet modern problem? As Mart De Haan continues his conversation with Avner and Nizar, you'll begin to get a refreshing and encouraging perspective, perhaps a new way of looking at how to think about the two people groups these men represent.

Can We Be Friends?

DAYLIGHT PREVIEW

Does God Take Sides?

Hope. It doesn't seem like a word that would be associated with the ongoing conflict in the Middle East between Jewish people and Arab people. But when you listen to Avner Boskey and Nizar Touma, you begin to sense that there is reason for hope. These two sons of Abraham represent two sides of the family that can't seem to get along, yet they see a way out. They sense that if people could understand what God wants—for all to call him "Our Father," for instance—there could be an opportunity for unity. It's less a question of whether God takes sides and more a question of who is on God's side.

COME TOGETHER

Icebreaker Questions

1. What are some situations you recall when you prayed the Lord's Prayer?

2. When it comes to observing situations of conflict, how quick are you to take sides?

3. On a scale of 1 (not at all) to 10 (all the time), how much do you enjoy discussing politics?

FINDING DAYLIGHT

Experience the Video

Feel free to jot down Video Notes as you watch the presentation by Mart De Haan, Avner Boskey, and Nizar Touma. Use the space below for those notes.

VIDEO NOTES

Avner Boskey and Nizar Touma

Can Christians love Jews and Arabs?

"God does not take sides"

The Bible: What God is up to

Issues of justice—relating to Abraham

A matter of humility

What if Christians from the West side with Israel politically?

What if Christians from the West support the Arab cause?

Mart's comments about partiality

The human issues

Avner: Dealing with the hearts of men

Nizar: Church standing with unredeemed Israel

Question: Is God restoring the Jewish people to the land?

The Lord's Prayer

Mart's conclusion

 WALKING IN THE DAYLIGHT

Discussion Time

DISCOVER GOD'S WORD

Discussion/Application Questions

1. Mart De Haan poses the following question at the beginning of
    this session: Is it possible for followers of Christ to be friends—real
    friends—to both Palestinian and Arab people *and* Jewish people? Is
    that possible, or do the political realities force us to take one side or
    the other?

    How would you answer that question?

2. **Avner Boskey's response is that we have to see God's heart for each individual person. Rather than seeing other people, too often people just see movements, and then they hate those movements or hate different sides.**

   Do you have a tendency to fall into that pattern of stereotyping? Explain.

3. Do you agree with Nizar Touma that God does not take sides in general and that He does not take sides in regard to the Israeli-Arab conflict in particular?

4. **Avner seems to take exception somewhat to Nizar's perspective, citing the need to take into account the entirety of the Bible—though it leads, inevitably, to some tension. Avner's understanding is that God is up to a certain strategy that no one likes; that is, He's restoring the Jewish people to the Promised Land even though other people are also living there. One passage that Avner notes in that regard is Zechariah 14.**

   Read Zechariah 14:1–11. The prophecy in verse 4 regarding the Lord coming to the Mount of Olives was probably in view in Acts 1:10–12 when Jesus ascended from the Mount of Olives to heaven and two angels told His disciples that He would come back in the same way.

   a. Though there are various interpretations about what all the imagery in Zechariah 14 means, what do you think of Avner's point that this passage confirms that God continues to have a plan for the Jewish people, including their restoration to the Promised Land?

   b. Do you agree with Avner that in this passage concerning Jesus' return, Jesus himself "takes a side"?

5. **Nizar feels that great damage is done to his ministry when his fellow Palestinians hear that Christians in America, and Christians who come to visit the Holy Land, are on Israel's side politically. He explains that it makes Palestinian born-again believers appear to be, by association, Zionists. Other Palestinians don't understand why European and American Christians come and stand with Israel rather than with their Christian brothers and sisters.**

How would you respond to Nizar's concern—to his sense even of betrayal? Does that affect how you think American Christians should support Israel?

6. **Mart states, "When followers of Christ show a prejudicial love for either Jewish or Arab people, rather than a heart of justice and mercy for both, such partiality ends up misrepresenting the true love of Christ for all."**

How can we flesh out and apply Mart's exhortation?

7. **Nizar expresses a concern about the church in America and Europe standing with Israel since Israel currently is not redeemed. Rather than political action, Nizar would seem to advocate instead that the church in America and Europe should focus on prayer.**

How would you respond to that?

8. **This session ends with Mart, Avner, and Nizar reciting the Lord's Prayer:**

   Our Father who art in heaven, hallowed be your name.
   Your kingdom come, your will be done on earth as it is in heaven.
   Give us this day our daily bread.
   And forgive us our trespasses, as we forgive those who trespass against us.
   And lead us not into temptation, but deliver us from evil.
   For yours is the kingdom, the power, and the glory forever. Amen.

   What insights does Jesus' model prayer provide in regard to our perspective—and perhaps even more importantly, in regard to our attitude—about the Jewish-Arab conflict?

BRINGING IT HOME

1. **Nizar points out the importance of humility—in his case, that Palestinian believers have to be humble in order to bless their Jewish friends and Jewish brothers.**

   Are there individuals or groups that require you to have more humility in order to bless them?

2. Avner notes a similar challenge: an attitude that says, "Okay, God, what is your heart for the Arab nations? Are you willing that they should perish? What is your heart for the Jewish nation? Are you willing that they should perish?"

Second Peter 3:9 states that God is patient, "not wanting anyone to perish, but everyone to come to repentance." How would your attitudes change if you were more like God in that respect?

 ## DAYLIGHT ON PRAYER

Spending Time with God

1. This session presents a call to prayer in regard to the Jewish-Arab conflict. Allow plenty of time to do that together as a group. Spend time, as well, praying for the salvation of people in your own community.

2. What other prayer concerns would you like the group to pray about?

3. Conclude by praying the Lord's Prayer together.

DAYLIGHT AHEAD

Do you like old buildings? Interesting buildings with a story to tell? In Session 3, you'll travel with Mart De Haan, Avner Boskey, and Nizar Touma to a battle-worn building on the border between Israel and Jordan to discuss the idea of peace in a world of conflict. What are we to think of the peace process in the Middle East? Avner and Nizar discuss that issue with Mart as they stand in that building with a fascinating map of the ancient Crusades as their backdrop.

Is Peace Possible?

DAYLIGHT PREVIEW

Prophetic Chess Game

What is happening in Israel? Some people, Avner Boskey suggests, look at the events in this land of conflict as either affirming or not affirming their own view of prophecy—and therefore they don't necessarily want peace. Instead, they want their view to be verified, even if it means bad things might happen. But how does "Pray for the peace of Jerusalem" work into this picture of what might be seen as a huge prophetic chess game?

—————— COME TOGETHER ——————

Icebreaker Questions

1. In this session we will take a look at a map that a bored Israeli soldier painted on the inside wall of a building. What do you do when you're bored? Are you a doodler? What's your most prized doodle?

2. What is the most "artistic" aspect of your personality and talents?

3. Avner Boskey compares end-time prophecy to a huge prophetic chess game. Any chess players in the group? What's the appeal?

FINDING DAYLIGHT

Experience the Video

Feel free to jot down Video Notes as you watch the presentation by Mart De Haan, Avner Boskey, and Nizar Touma. Use the space below for those notes.

────────────── VIDEO NOTES──────────────

Abandoned building

Avner Boskey and Nizar Touma

History and geography of the building

The wall—Crusader map

Today's map of the Middle East

The peace process and Christians

False peace and Israel

Ultimate peace

WALKING IN THE DAYLIGHT

Discussion Time

———————— DISCOVER GOD'S WORD ————————
Discussion/Application Questions

1. **After looking at the Crusader map in the abandoned building near Israel's border with Jordan, Mart De Haan reflects that today's map of the Middle East is anything but peaceful.**

    a. Why do you think so many of the nations around Israel feel the way they do about Israel?

    b. How do you feel about the way Israel handles this situation?

2. Why do you think Christians, as Mart has noticed over the years, are often very suspicious of the peace process in the Middle East—to the point that at times it almost seems like peace is bad news?

3. **Avner Boskey develops this situation further by noting that some people, unfortunately, see biblical prophecy as just a huge prophetic chess game. "And so they're thinking, 'Where are the players and how's it all going to work out?' And often there's even a bloodthirstiness involved in it, where people are saying, 'You know, this has to work out bad so that I will have my game won properly.' "**

Can you relate to Avner's observation that the end result of this thinking is an attitude leaning toward "The worse it gets, the happier I feel"?

4. **Seeing that attitude as an abuse of what God is doing and of how we should respond as believers, Avner points to 1 Timothy 2. Read 1 Timothy 2:1–4.**

   a. How does this passage speak to the attitude we should have regarding politics and governing authorities in general?

   b. How does this passage speak to the attitude we should have regarding the Jewish-Arab conflict in particular?

5. **Avner also points to Psalm 122. Read that psalm.**

What does it mean for us today to "Pray for the peace of Jerusalem" (v. 6)? Do we need to pray with a specific agenda—or should we simply call out to our Father ("Your kingdom come, Your will be done") and let Him take it from there?

6. While affirming that Jesus gives us, as individual believers, peace through having a relationship with the Lord, Nizar states that the peace we have in our hearts is not the full idea or full concept of peace. Ultimate peace, the peace that will bring the conflict in the Middle East to an end, is something special that only God can provide. Read Isaiah 2:1–5, one of the biblical prophecies that pictures ultimate peace.

    a. What elements of this prophecy could be produced only by God?

    b. Are we responsible to take any steps toward this picture of ultimate peace? If so, what might they be?

BRINGING IT HOME

Jesus taught us to pray, "Your kingdom come, your will be done on earth as it is in heaven" (Matthew 6:10). Although ultimate peace won't come until God's kingdom comes in its fullness, we can have peace within our hearts. Jesus promised, "Peace I leave with you; my peace I give you. I do not give to you as the world gives. Do not let your hearts be troubled and do not be afraid" (John 14:27).

To what extent are you experiencing Christ's peace? Are there situations that are causing you to be troubled or afraid?

DAYLIGHT ON PRAYER

Spending Time with God

1. How can the group pray for you in light of what you just shared?

2. What other requests would you like to share with the group?

3. Spend some time as a group responding to the injunction found in Psalm 122:6: "Pray for the peace of Jerusalem."

DAYLIGHT AHEAD

As Mart De Haan, Avner Boskey, and Nizar Touma stand in a building that has suffered wartime bombardment, they continue to discuss peace. Is it possible, Mart asks, for peace to be found in Israel—or are there just going to be episodes of "false peace," as he calls them? Do peace treaties change hearts? Or is there something that leads to a deeper acceptance of each other? These and other vital questions are pursued in this meeting of three Christian friends: one American, one Arab, and one Jewish.

Peacemakers and the Human Heart

DAYLIGHT PREVIEW

False Peace and the Mideast

When Mart De Haan, Avner Boskey, and Nizar Touma discuss peace while standing before the backdrop of a bombed-out building, they refer to a number of kinds of peace. Personal peace. Societal peace. Promised peace. And an occasional false peace. How can one know what is true peace and what is false? Is it peace in the heart or is it peace on paper? Does it come from human leaders or is there another source? And can believers in Jesus be peacemakers when cultures lack peace between each other? A warm relationship between three very different men indicate that it can happen.

COME TOGETHER

Icebreaker Questions

1. When you were growing up, how often did a third party have to enforce a "peace treaty" or truce upon you and a sibling or you and a playmate?

2. Mart De Haan notes that Nizar Touma probably has some Arab brothers and sisters who would resent the fact that he is expressing affection for Jewish people. Have you ever taken some heat from your own "people" for your relationship with someone from another group?

SESSION 4—Peacemakers and the Human Heart   33

3. Name one person you admire as a true peacemaker.

 FINDING DAYLIGHT

Experience the Video

Feel free to jot down Video Notes as you watch the presentation by Mart De Haan, Avner Boskey, and Nizar Touma. Use the space below for those notes.

―――――――――――――――― VIDEO NOTES ―――――――――――

Peace and the community

The danger of false peace

Can we be peacemakers before Jesus returns?

What about resentment of others?

Land and people: The Abrahamic covenant

Nizar: "Is that God's heart?"

Attitude toward peace

Government peace?

Mart: Peacemakers at heart

WALKING IN THE DAYLIGHT

Discussion Time

DISCOVER GOD'S WORD

Discussion/Application Questions

1. **In this session, as well as the previous session, Mart De Haan raises a concern about a future false peace.**

   What do you think about Mart's observation that a lot of people think the Bible teaches that in the last days there is going to be an anti-Messiah, or anti-Christ, figure who will forge a false peace on the Middle East, and therefore those people tend to be very suspicious of any peace that begins to be promoted today?

2. **Avner Boskey and Nizar Touma state that they are concerned— beyond peace treaties and peace movements—about what is really going on within people's hearts.**

   How much do you share their concern?

3. What does Mart mean when he says that we can't wish for peace at any price in the Arab-Jewish conflict because we know that justice is an issue?

4. **In light of the fact, as Mart says, that we don't believe there will be ultimate peace in the Middle East or in the world until God himself has His way—until the Messiah comes and rules—can we be peace-makers in the meantime? Can we hope for and work for something short of that—something that says to others, "We value right rela-tionships not only with our God but with one another, and not only between Christian and Christian, but between neighbors—regardless of our faith"?**

   How can we help make those things happen?

5. What impresses you about the "warm peace," as Avner calls it, between Avner and Nizar—"two sons of Abraham that God has made peace between"? What allows Avner and Nizar to be peacemakers at heart?

What can we learn from them that can be applied even in relationships among people in our churches?

6. **Avner refers to Isaiah 19. Although Israel is still called God's inheritance, there is a lot of warmth in God's heart for everybody in the Middle East, as pictured in the image of a highway running through the region. Read Isaiah 19:19–25.**

   a. For centuries the Egyptians and Assyrians had been enemies of Israel and of each other. What will eventually link them together in a bond of friendship?

   b. How do you suppose the Israelites who comprised Isaiah's original audience felt about this prophecy?

   c. How would you expect Israelis and their neighbors to feel about this prophecy today?

7. Although, as Avner says, we can't put a lot of trust in governmental processes of peace, what expectations and hopes should we have for governments being able to establish a certain amount of peace and tranquility?

8. **In the last session we reflected on 1 Timothy 2:1–4. Read those verses again.**

How does this passage speak to the question of appropriate expectations and hopes for governments being able to establish a certain amount of peace and tranquility?

—————————————— BRINGING IT HOME ——————————————

The Scriptures call us to be peacemakers:

"Blessed are the peacemakers, for they will be called sons of God." (Matthew 5:9)

"Let us therefore make every effort to do what leads to peace and to mutual edification." (Romans 14:19)

"Peacemakers who sow in peace raise a harvest of righteousness." (James 3:18)

Where, and how, do you sense that God is wanting to use you as a peacemaker—for example, in your family, at work, at church, in your neighborhood, in your community or city, in a broader sense (such as the Arab-Jewish conflict)?

 ## DAYLIGHT ON PRAYER

Spending Time with God

1. Use 1 Timothy 2:1–4 as a guide to pray for Israel and the Middle East, as well as for your own nation and governmental officials.

2. Avner comments, "If an Arab and a Jew can relate to each other, and two Arabs and two Jews can relate to each other, and then we can begin to show that love in each one of our communities, that can start kind of a ripple effect." Pray for the kind of ripple effect that would happen if more Jews and Arabs would relate to each other like Avner and Nizar now do.

3. Do you have any personal prayer requests to share with the group?

DAYLIGHT AHEAD

The three Christian brothers—one American, one Jewish, and one Arab—meet again. This time they have traveled to Jerusalem to discuss a topic that would seem to ensure tension between the Jewish and Arab friends: God chose the Jewish people as a "special treasure" and not the Arab people. How fair is this? How can it not cause automatic tension? The three discuss the implications of the fact that God singled out the Jews as His chosen people.

A Chosen People: Is This Fair?

DAYLIGHT PREVIEW

Nobody's Happy

Who has not seen Tevye in *Fiddler on the Roof* as he cries out to God, "We are your chosen people. Once in a while, can't you choose someone else?" Avner Boskey echoes that sentiment as he discusses the "chosen" concept with Mart De Haan. And Nizar Touma says his people often wonder why it was the other guys, not his Arab brothers and sisters, who were God's chosen. It seems that nobody's happy with the arrangement. In an honest exchange between the two men, it's easy to see why this one factor has long been a difficult subject to deal with in real life.

———————————— COME TOGETHER ————————————

Icebreaker Questions

1. When the kids on the playground picked teams, how soon were you usually chosen? How did that make you feel?

2. Are you a fan of *Fiddler on the Roof*? If so, what do you like best about it?

3. Avner Boskey points out that parental discipline is valuable and to be expected. How did you feel about your parents' discipline when you were growing up? Looking back, if you could have changed anything, what would you change?

 ## FINDING DAYLIGHT

Experience the Video

Feel free to jot down Video Notes as you watch the presentation by Mart De Haan, Avner Boskey, and Nizar Touma. Use the space below for those notes.

———— VIDEO NOTES ————

A chosen people? How far apart are Nizar and Avner?

Fiddler on the Roof quote: Nobody's happy about it

Does God play favorites?

The pain of being chosen

How do Arabs respond to Avner's concept?

Avner and the idea of being "chosen"

The calling: Not favoritism

WALKING IN THE DAYLIGHT

Discussion Time

DISCOVER GOD'S WORD

Discussion/Application Questions

1. Mart De Haan begins this session by stating that one of the difficult questions raised by the Bible is how an impartial God can have a "chosen people."

   What do you think?

2. **Mart then alludes to Deuteronomy 7:6. Compare these words of Moses with those he spoke earlier, at Mount Sinai, as recorded in Exodus 19:5–6.**

   a.   What condition is added to Moses' statement in Exodus 19:5–6?

   b.   How significant do you think that condition is?

3. It's no surprise that Nizar Touma reports that his fellow Arabs wonder why God would choose a people and why He would choose the Jewish people rather than other peoples. But were you surprised that Avner said his fellow Jews ask the same question?

   What do you make of the common attitude among Jews that they have been chosen for the nations to hate them and to be against them?

4. **Avner notes that we first see God's plan to use one family line as a blessing for all people in Genesis 3, when God speaks to Satan (the serpent) after Adam and Eve sinned. Read Genesis 3:12–15.**

   How does the rest of the Bible, as it follows Adam and Eve's descendants through the nation of Israel, unpack this prophecy about destroying the works of Satan?

5. **Avner then refers to Genesis 12:1–3 as additional evidence that God, in His strategy to destroy the works of Satan on earth, chose the Jewish people. Read those verses.**

   a. Why do both Jews and Christians view this as a watershed passage in regard to human history?

   b. How do you suppose this passage is viewed by Arabs—since they also see themselves as children of Abraham?

6. What do you think of Avner's comparison of Israel to the firstborn son who gets double the inheritance of all the other sons but is also doubly responsible?

7. **Avner sees a connection between this concept of the firstborn son and Paul's words in Romans 2. Read Romans 2:9–11.**

   a. Do you agree with Avner that this passage says that in the day of judgment the Jewish people are going to get twice as much judgment and twice as much reward?

   b. Do you agree with Avner that this passage says that the calling of Israel is not actually favoritism?

—————————————— BRINGING IT HOME ——————————————

1. **When Nizar observes that Jews are unhappy that they were chosen, while other people are wishing that they were chosen, Avner responds, "The grass is always greener on the other side."**

    a. How much trouble do you have with thinking the grass is always greener on the other side of the fence?

    b. Similarly, how much do you struggle with feeling that God plays favorites—and you're not one of them?

2. **Avner points out that both the Jewish people and Christian believers are disciplined by God to keep them humble. Hebrews 12:6 says that "the Lord disciplines those he loves." Furthermore, "Our fathers disciplined us for a little while as they thought best; but God disciplines us for our good, that we may share in his holiness" (Hebrews 12:10).**

    How might this principle affect your view of God, especially if you feel like you're not one of His "favorites"?

DAYLIGHT ON PRAYER

Spending Time with God

1. If you're feeling like life, or God, isn't fair, express that to God. Then ask for His intervention, discernment, and guidance. Perhaps this calls for silent prayer.

2. If your heart is filled with gratitude, express your thanks and praise to God—the giver of "every good and perfect gift" (James 1:17).

3. How can the group support you, or your concerns for others, in prayer?

DAYLIGHT AHEAD

The fact that the Jews are God's chosen people goes beyond theory and doctrine, notes Mart De Haan as he talks to Nizar Touma and Avner Boskey about this difficult, volatile subject. It is made stickier because it is also about the land where the three are walking: the Promised Land of Israel. Israel claims it. The Palestinians claim it. What should people do about it? Whose land is it? With caring and compassion, the men discuss this key issue.

Whose Land Is This?

DAYLIGHT PREVIEW

A Refreshing View

While the battle over the land of Israel continues to go on, is it possible to come up with a diplomatic, calm way to look at the problem? Maybe so, say Avner Boskey and Nizar Touma. If both sides were to see their roles in God's family as calling them to care for and have compassion for the others, many of the issues that divide could be issues that bring people together. As Nizar suggests, then perhaps Israel could be a blessing to others in the world community.

COME TOGETHER

Icebreaker Questions

1. Did the oldest child in your family take a lot of responsibility for the younger siblings? How about in the case of your own children?

2. What is the closest you have come to experiencing a struggle for land or real estate?

3. Avner Boskey refers to God as a "multitasker." How good are you at multitasking?

FINDING DAYLIGHT

Experience the Video

Feel free to jot down Video Notes as you watch the presentation by Mart De Haan, Nizar Touma, and Avner Boskey. Use the space below for those notes.

─────────────────────VIDEO NOTES─────────────────────

The oldest son concept

Jacob have I loved . . .

What about the Promised Land?

Should an Arab give up his ancestral land?

God is restoring the Jewish people to the land

God the multitasker

The challenge: Prophecy and compassion

Chosen: Not superiority, but responsibility

Jews: To be a blessing

Christians: Jews and Arabs as brothers

Nizar: The view from the outside in

Avner: Praying for what makes for peace

Faith and Jesus' crucifixion

Mart's summary

WALKING IN THE DAYLIGHT

Discussion Time

————————————DISCOVER GOD'S WORD————————————

Discussion/Application Questions

1. The first chapter of Malachi includes a statement that, according to Avner Boskey, "makes theologians crazy"! Read Malachi 1:1–3.

   The two brothers here, Esau and Jacob, were Isaac and Rebekah's twin sons. Esau, the older brother, became the father of the Edomites. Jacob, whom God later renamed Israel, became the father of the Israelites. Read Romans 9:10–13, where Paul quotes Malachi 1:2–3 in illustrating the doctrine of election.

   Perhaps a legitimate way to restate "Jacob I loved, but Esau I hated" would be "Jacob I chose, but Esau I rejected."

   Mart De Haan states that chosenness, if we understand it correctly according to the Scriptures, is not an issue of favoritism or partiality. Do you believe that holds true even for this rather remarkable statement in Malachi 1:2–3 and Romans 9:13?

2. Avner thinks it is important to contrast this situation with God's blessing on Ishmael. Read about that blessing, which was part of a story in which the Lord appeared to Abraham, in Genesis 17:15–22. Ishmael was thirteen years old at this time.

What evidence is there in this passage for Avner's perspective that although God's chosen strategy was through Isaac, this was not an either-or situation?

3. How would you respond to Nizar Touma when he asks, "How can you blame me for being born here—for being a citizen of this country? What do I have to do? Should I just give up my rights for this land, which is the land of my ancestors?"

4. **In response to Mart's question regarding whether we know that God is restoring the Jewish people to the Promised Land based on Bible prophecy, Avner refers to Isaiah 11:11. Read that verse.**

   Some Bible scholars point out that the first time God reclaimed a remnant was when He brought the Israelites out of Egypt (see Isaiah 11:16), and that the "second time" would likely be when some Israelites returned from Assyrian and Babylonian exile. The basis for Avner's view is strong, however, since the verses prior to verse 11 clearly point to the messianic age.

   a. Assuming this passage does refer to God restoring the Jewish people to the land in the end times, how would you answer Mart's next question: "Is the implication that everyone who is not Jewish should be getting out at this point?"

   b. How do you feel about Avner's response: "You're asking a question that really can't be answered today, because it's in the process of being answered"?

5. Avner goes on to state that Ezekiel 36 and 37 demonstrate the covenant God made between the land and the Jewish people. Nizar notes that Ezekiel also talks about a time when the Jews would be in the land along with strangers. Read about that in Ezekiel 47:21–23.

   Though interpretations of the last part of the book of Ezekiel vary greatly, how does the spirit of this passage speak to the current Jewish-Arab conflict?

6. Avner also comments that the Scriptures call for the people of Israel to be both a light and a servant to the nations. To look at the issue of chosenness with any sense of superiority of Jews over Arabs, consequently, is to twist what chosenness means. In fact, Avner says, "I am created to serve the Arab people, to bless them, to love them, and to prefer them above myself."

   a. How common do you suppose that attitude is among Israelis today?

   b. What would that attitude mean, practically speaking, in regard to the Jewish-Arab conflict—particularly in respect to the land?

7. What do you think of Nizar's exhortation that, in light of the fact that God is a just God and we are outsiders, we should resist taking the side of either the Palestinians or the Jews—and instead we should

pray that we will see in the best way how God can bring these two peoples together so they can dwell together in the land?

BRINGING IT HOME

Nizar admits that before he became a true follower of Jesus he thought he should hate the Jews because they crucified Jesus. But when he came to faith he realized he couldn't blame the Jews, or anyone else, for doing that. The blame for Jesus' death rightly belongs to our sins. "And," Nizar adds, "I probably blame myself first that He went to the cross."

Nizar recognized that he needed God to deal with his heart in regard to how he should love the people around him—especially his "enemies," the people who weren't like him.

> Does God need to deal with your heart in regard to how you should love the people around you? If so, how could Nizar's humility about his own sins serve as a helpful example for you?

 DAYLIGHT ON PRAYER

Spending Time with God

1. In response to Nizar's challenge (see Question 7), pray that you will see the best way for God to bring the Jews and Arabs together so that they can dwell together in the land.

2. Spend some time praying for concerns in your own life as well as for burdens you have for others.

DAYLIGHT AHEAD

The land. As Mart, Avner, and Nizar walk along the dusty roads of a desolate part of Israel, it's not hard to imagine a time when the land was occupied only by scattered groups of people. In the long period between the destruction of the temple in 70 AD and the return of the nation of Israel in 1948, people of all kinds lived in the land and raised generations of families. So how is this all worked out? Jews returning. Arabs in the land. It's a problem of ownership. A "clash," as Nizar calls it. What is the church to think?

"The Wild West Bank"

DAYLIGHT PREVIEW

Replacement Theology

When the Jewish people were disbursed—when they were ousted from Jer-susalem, was that God's idea? Was that what He wanted? Was it His idea to replace the Jewish people with a new entity, the church, as His new chosen people? It's a concept some embrace, so Mart, Avner, and Nizar discuss the history that led up to that idea.

―――――――――――― COME TOGETHER ――――――――――――

Icebreaker Questions

1. Have you ever had a cat who loved to roam? What was the longest time he or she was gone before returning home?

2. How many generations of your family have lived in this country? How many generations of your family have lived in the area where you grew up?

3. Avner Boskey notes that sometimes the Jewish people have served as a good example and other times they have served as a bad example. Who served as a good example for you when you were a kid? Who served as a bad example?

 FINDING DAYLIGHT

Experience the Video

Feel free to jot down Video Notes as you watch the presentation by Mart De Haan, Avner Boskey, and Nizar Touma. Use the space below for those notes.

────────────────── VIDEO NOTES ──────────────────

"The cat comes back." Jewish people in and out of the land

Generational homeland of many

Replacement theology

Have the Jews forfeited the land?

Sin and grace

Why did God bring the Jews back into the land?

Good example, bad example

 WALKING IN THE DAYLIGHT

Discussion Time

DISCOVER GOD'S WORD

Discussion/Application Questions

1. For the most part, the Jews maintained only a remnant presence in the Holy Land from the time of the Roman destruction of Jerusalem in 70 AD until the restoration of national Israel in 1948. Meanwhile, some Arab people have lived in the land continuously since the Arab invasion in 638 AD.

   Do these realities affect your perspective about the Jewish-Arab conflict in regard to the land?

2. Why do many Christians believe that the Jewish people have forfeited their right to the land?

3. Avner Boskey offers the following characterization of those who advocate what is sometimes called "replacement theology." "They say that because Jewish people have sinned, God has lost patience with them. He doesn't like them anymore. His intention was never to continue working with them, and He couldn't wait for the chance to dump them and embrace the Gentiles, whom He loves a lot more."

   a. How common do you think that perspective is?

   b. Why do you think Avner feels so strongly about this subject?

4. Mart De Haan puts a far more positive spin on what Avner calls replacement theology. He envisions God, with a broken heart, saying to the Jews, "You have turned your back on Me, and this is the occasion now for Me to draw men and women from every nation into one body of Messiah."

   How consistent do you think that scenario is with the Scriptures?

5. Many Christians have identified a number of New Testament passages that seem to point to followers of Jesus, both Jews and Gentiles, as the "new Israel"—not necessarily replacing national Israel but fulfilling God's spiritual plan for all people. Here are some of

those key texts, all of which were written to churches comprised of at least some, if not a majority of, Gentile believers:

- Galatians 3:28–29: "There is neither Jew nor Greek, slave nor free, male nor female, for you are all one in Christ Jesus. If you belong to Christ, then you are Abraham's seed, and heirs according to the promise."

- Galatians 6:16: "Peace and mercy to all who follow this rule, even to the Israel of God."

- Philippians 3:3: "It is we who are the circumcision, we who worship by the Spirit of God, who glory in Christ Jesus, and who put no confidence in the flesh."

- 1 Peter 2:9–10: "You are a chosen people, a royal priesthood, a holy nation, a people belonging to God, that you may declare the praises of him who called you out of darkness into his wonderful light. Once you were not a people, but now you are the people of God; once you had not received mercy, but now you have received mercy."

a. What continuities do you see between these verses and descriptions of the Jewish people in the Old Testament?

b. Can we value Scriptures like these without also embracing the kind of replacement theology Avner fears?

c. What effect, if any, do you think Scriptures like this should have on the Jewish-Arab conflict and conversations?

6. Avner notes that in Deuteronomy 28 the Lord guarantees that He will evict the people of Israel from the Promised Land for violating His law and breaking the Mosaic covenant. But then Avner sees something quite different in Deuteronomy 30. Read Deuteronomy 30:1–10.

   a. Avner views this passage as being fulfilled "at the end of time," presumably in the days before Christ's second coming. What evidence do you see for that as opposed to, say, the Israelites returning to the Promised Land after the Babylonian exile?

   b. Do you agree with Avner that the grace promised in Deuteronomy 30 reflects a covenant other than the Mosaic covenant?

——————————— BRINGING IT HOME ———————————

Avner believes that God, in a sense, is offending the minds of people by bringing the Jewish people back to the Promised Land. He thinks this is difficult even for a lot of Christians because so much theology has been a denial that God could have mercy and grace for the Jewish people again.

Avner also sees the Jews as a type, or example, for all people in this regard. Avner asks, "How do we deal with our own sin? And do we believe God can really forgive us and use us again?"

How much have you wrestled with believing God can really forgive you?

Is that a reality that is holding you back from growing spiritually and using your gifts?

DAYLIGHT ON PRAYER

Spending Time with God

1. Spend some time in silent prayer reflecting on your sin and God's grace. If you need to, ask God for His forgiveness. Be confident in accepting His forgiveness. Invite God to use you for the sake of His kingdom.

2. How can the group pray for you and join you in praying for other concerns?

DAYLIGHT AHEAD

So, what is the plan God has for Israel? Avner Boskey and Nizar Touma will continue to tackle this subject as Session 8 begins. How are Christians to read the prophesies about Israel? Nizar explains the important concept that all who belong to God were chosen by Him.

A Beautiful Picture:
One Flock—One Shepherd

 DAYLIGHT PREVIEW

Grace and Mystery

As a result of the gift of salvation through Christ—through His grace—a mystery takes place. People of all nations are grafted together as one. But does that mean the church "becomes" Israel? And how does a Christian Arab present Jesus—a Jew—to his own people as the Messiah? All of these questions are important, but what is most important is that salvation is a beautiful picture: God took people from all nations and turned them into one flock under one Shepherd.

——————————— **COME TOGETHER** ———————————
Icebreaker Questions

1. In this session Avner Boskey mentions chopped liver. Are there any Jewish foods that you really like? What is your favorite ethnic food (other than your own)?

2. In this session we see how the apostle Paul uses the image of an olive tree. Were you much of a tree-climber when you were a kid?

3. At the end of this session, Nizar Touma and Avner Boskey remark that "Different can be beautiful." If you are married, how are you and your spouse the most alike? How are you the most different?

FINDING DAYLIGHT

Experience the Video

Feel free to jot down Video Notes as you watch the presentation by Mart De Haan, Nizar Touma, and Avner Boskey. Use the space below for those notes.

---VIDEO NOTES---

Times of the Gentiles

God's heart and being chosen

The remnant

Church vs. Israel

Arabs and a Jewish Messiah

The olive tree

The roots and the branches

Jews and Arabs: How can we believe?

Continuity on the calling of Israel

The beautiful picture

WALKING IN THE DAYLIGHT

Discussion Time

——————————— DISCOVER GOD'S WORD ———————————

Discussion/Application Questions

1. Referring to Ephesians 3, Avner Boskey states that all Gentile believers are brought into the commonwealth of Israel, although this doesn't mean they are Jews. **Read Ephesians 3:1–6.**

   a. If Gentile believers in Jesus don't become Jews, do they share equal standing with the Jewish believers who are part of this one new "body"?

   b. The "mystery" that Paul refers to would seem to apply in a special way to Jewish and Arab believers like Avner Boskey and Nizar Touma coming together in unity. What two groups in your community would really express this mystery?

2. Nizar points out how it takes much humility for an Arab to receive a Messiah who was a Jew. Likewise, Avner points out how hard it is for Jews to believe in Jesus because He has become the Gentile God. In either case, one's identity is challenged.

   What identity challenges are there for people in our culture who are considering becoming followers of Jesus?

3. **In Romans 11, Paul uses the image of an olive tree in his discussion of the relationship between Jews and Gentiles. Read Romans 11:11–24.**

   a. How would salvation coming to the Gentiles make the Jews envious (v. 11).

   b. Why would the Jews' transgression mean riches for the world (v. 12)?

   c. Why did the wild olive shoot (Gentile believers) have no business boasting over the branches (Jews) that had been broken off (vv. 17–21)?

   d. What will it take for the broken-off branches to be grafted in again (vv. 23–24)?

4. **Mart De Haan raises the question of how we should answer someone who says, "How do we know that this talk of a Promised Land or a future for Israel is not something of the past? It's gone the way of the old covenant; it's gone the way of the temple and the sacrifices and the priesthood. And now today we've got this new wonderful international body of Messiah, which is so much better than the old."**

   How would you respond to that question?

5. **Avner's response is to turn again to Romans 11. Read Romans 11:1–6.**

    Though Paul is clear that God has not rejected His people, the Jews, do you agree with Avner that there is also clear continuity in regard to God's promises to national Israel and the land?

6. **Avner then refers to a key verse, Romans 11:29. Consider that verse in its context by reading Romans 11:25–32.**

    What do you think it means for the Jews today that "God's gifts and his call are irrevocable" (v. 29)? Again, do you agree with Avner that this promise pertains to national Israel and the land?

7. **Nizar alludes to Jesus' words in John 10:16: "I have other sheep that are not of this sheep pen. I must bring them also. They too will listen to my voice, and there shall be one flock and one shepherd." This is a beautiful picture of Jews and Gentiles together under one shepherd, Jesus.**

    When are differences between people beautiful? When are they ugly?

8. **Nizar observes that there is a lot of common ground between believers, and that even in the case of a Palestinian believer and a Jewish believer there is more to agree about than to be divided about.**

Summarizing the Jewish-Arab conflict, then, Mart says, "Having discussed the complexities of it, it seems like we can come out together with a very simple answer: that what God does will be good; and what God does will be good for all who accept Him, who bow the knee to His Son; and that when this difficult drama plays out in its fullness there won't be anyone who trusts God who will say, 'You've done a bad thing. You've been unfair to me. You haven't given me the land that I need for my family, the land that I need or the food that I need or the security that I need.' God is a good God."

How do you feel about that summary? Would you add anything to it?

BRINGING IT HOME

1. Has your perspective regarding the conflict between the Jewish and Palestinian people changed during this study? If so, how?

2. Mart concludes by saying that the real matter for all of us is "Will we let God be God, not only in the Middle East but in our own hearts—in my heart?"

How forcefully can you answer that question in the affirmative? Does anything keep you from saying yes with more conviction?

DAYLIGHT ON PRAYER

Spending Time with God

1. What have you appreciated the most about this series and about this group?

2. How can the group continue to support you in prayer?